Science Fair Projects About Rocks and Minerals

Robert Gardner

 Enslow Publishing
101 W. 23rd Street
Suite 240
New York, NY 10011
USA

enslow.com

Published in 2017 by Enslow Publishing, LLC.
101 W. 23rd Street, Suite 240, New York, NY 10011

Library of Congress Cataloging-in-Publication Data

Names: Gardner, Robert, 1929– author.
Title: Science fair projects about rocks and minerals / Robert Gardner.
Description: New York, NY : Enslow Publishing, 2017. | Series: Hands-on science | Audience: Ages 8+. | Audience: Grades 4 to 6. | Includes bibliographical references and index.
Identifiers: LCCN 2016019994| ISBN 9780766082090 (library bound) | ISBN 9780766082274 (pbk.) | ISBN 9780766082083 (6-pack)
Subjects: LCSH: Minerals—Experiments—Juvenile literature. | Rocks—Experiments—Juvenile literature. | Science projects—Juvenile literature.
Classification: LCC QE432.2 .G37 2017 | DDC 549.078—dc23
LC record available at https://lccn.loc.gov/2016019994

Printed in China

To Our Readers: We have done our best to make sure all website addresses in this book were active and appropriate when we went to press. However, the author and the publisher have no control over and assume no liability for the material available on those websites or on any websites they may link to. Any comments or suggestions can be sent by email to customerservice@enslow.com.

Portions of this book originally appeared in the book *Smashing Science Projects About Earth's Rocks and Minerals* by Robert Gardner.

Photo Credits: Cover, p. 1 Triff/Shutterstock.com (colorful stones); Barry Tuck/ Shutterstock.com (sedimentary rock on back cover); Strejman/Shutterstock. com (handprint on spine); design elements throughout book: ctrlaplus/ Shutterstock.com (quote bubbles), Bimbim/Shutterstock.com (science doodles in blue background), Sergey Nivens/Shutterstock.com (lightbulb), Paul Velgos/ Shutterstock.com (notebook), StepanPopov/Shutterstock.com (question marks); p. 4 Zack Frank/Shutterstock.com.

Illustrations by Joseph Hill.

Contents

Introduction

We live on a huge amount of rocks and minerals that we call Earth. Many of the rocks we see today were once a hot liquid deep inside our planet. In this book, you will learn about rocks and minerals by doing experiments. You will discover that Earth is always changing. You will learn about different types of rocks and where they come from. You will see how soil is made from rocks and how crystals form in certain shapes. You will make models to see how rocks form and change. You will learn about all these things and much more.

Before each experiment in this book, you will be asked to write down your ideas about what you think might happen. Start a science notebook to record your ideas and results.

Entering a Science Fair

Some experiments in this book have ideas for science fair projects. However, judges at science fairs like experiments that are creative. So do not simply copy an experiment in this book. Pick one of the ideas suggested and develop a project of your own. Choose something you really like and want to know more about. It will be more interesting to you, and it can lead to a creative experiment that you plan and carry out.

Before entering a science fair, read one or more of the books listed under Further Reading. They will give you helpful hints and lots of useful information about science fairs.

Safety First

To do experiments safely, always follow these rules:

1 Do experiments **under adult supervision**.

2 Read all instructions carefully. If you have questions, **check with the adult**.

3 Be serious when experimenting. Fooling around can be dangerous to you and to others.

4 Keep the area where you work clean and organized. When you have finished, clean up and put all of your materials away.

What Are Minerals?

Things You Will Need:

- table salt
- clear piece of rigid plastic
- magnifying glass
- sugar
- sand
- Epsom salts

Minerals are inorganic. Inorganic means they do not come from living things. Each mineral has its own particular chemical makeup. What do you think small particles of minerals look like? Write down your ideas in your science notebook.

Let's Investigate!

1 Salt is a mineral. Shake a few grains of table salt onto a piece of clear plastic. Examine the particles with a magnifying glass. What do they look like?

2 Repeat the experiment with grains of sugar. Sugar comes from sugar cane, which is a plant. What do particles of sugar look like?

3 Repeat the experiment using grains of sand. What do particles of sand look like?

4 Repeat the process using Epsom salts (magnesium sulfate). What do particles of Epsom salts look like?

You looked at the particles of several different substances. Which one was not a mineral? Why wasn't it a mineral?

Salt, sand, or sugar

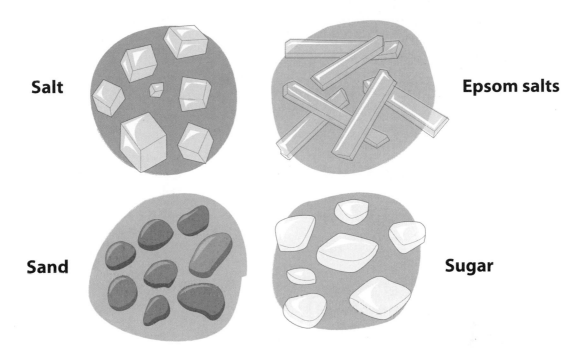

Salt

Epsom salts

Sand

Sugar

What Are Minerals? *The Facts*

Most of the magnified particles you saw were mineral crystals. Each crystal has a certain shape. But the shapes of the crystals you saw differed. Most of them were crystals that had been broken or worn down. The grains of sand might even have been round. They may have been smoothed by waves and flowing water.

Sugar is not a mineral because it is made by sugar cane, a living plant.

Rocks are usually mixtures of minerals. But some rocks were once living things. Coal is a rock made from plants that were once living. The dead plants slowly changed into coal over millions of years.

2

Can You Make Crystals?

Things You Will Need:

- measuring cup marked with fluid ounces
- measuring teaspoon
- spoon for stirring
- kosher salt
- drinking glasses
- warm tap water
- three shallow, clear, plastic dishes
- Epsom salts
- alum (from a pharmacy)
- magnifying glass
- pencil and paper

How could you make crystals? Write down your ideas and your reasons for them.

1 Pour two ounces of warm water into a drinking glass. Add a teaspoon of kosher salt. Stir with another spoon until all the salt dissolves. Continue to add salt until no more will dissolve after much stirring. Pour a little of the liquid into a shallow, clear, plastic dish. Carefully put the dish in a warm place. Write "kosher salt" on a small piece of paper and put it next to the dish.

2 Get some Epsom salts and a clean glass. Using clean spoons, repeat what you did before but using Epsom salts. Label this plastic dish "Epsom salts."

3 Get some alum and a clean glass. Using clean spoons, repeat what you did before but using alum. Label this dish "alum."

4 Look at the dishes every day. The water will disappear (evaporate) after a few days. What is left after the water evaporates?

5 Examine the solids that are left with a magnifying glass. Describe what you see. What do you think the solids are? How can you tell one solid from another just by looking?

Alum

Epsom salts

Kosher salt

Can You Make Crystals? *The Facts*

As the water evaporates (goes into the air), crystals of salt, Epsom salts, and alum appear. The crystals of each solid are different. Salt crystals (halite) look like cubes. Epsom salts crystals look like long rectangular columns. Alum crystals are diamond shaped. You can see that some crystals have joined together. One look tells you that the crystals of the three solids are different. Some scientists would be able to tell what the solids are just by looking at them.

Alum

Salt

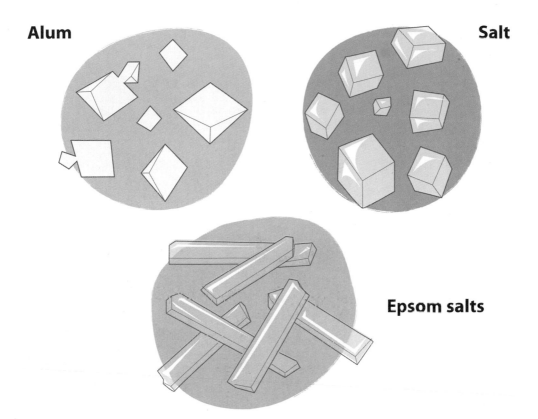

Epsom salts

Idea for Your Science Fair

● How can you grow large crystals from dissolved minerals? You can find books on the subject in your library. You might start with sugar (rock candy) and go on to alum, salt, and other minerals.

Where Can You Find Minerals?

- various items around your home or school

What minerals or things that contain minerals can you find around your home and school? Write down your ideas.

1. Look for minerals or things that contain minerals in your kitchen. (Hint: You already know that salt is a mineral, and so are metals.) If it did not come from an animal or a vegetable, it is probably a mineral. What minerals can you find? If you have difficulty, ask an adult to help you.

2. Can you find minerals or things that contain minerals in other places in your home? If you can, what are they?

3. Can you find minerals or things that contain minerals outside your home or at school? If you can, what are they?

What minerals can you find in your home?

Where Can You Find Minerals?
The Facts

There are lots of minerals or things that have minerals in them. You can find them inside and outside your home and school. Here are some that you may have found: salt, glass, silverware, chrome, ice, chalk, pencil lead (graphite and clay), diamonds, gold, silver, copper, coins, talcum powder, thumbtacks, paper clips, ceramics, nails, concrete, soil, jewelry, and so on.

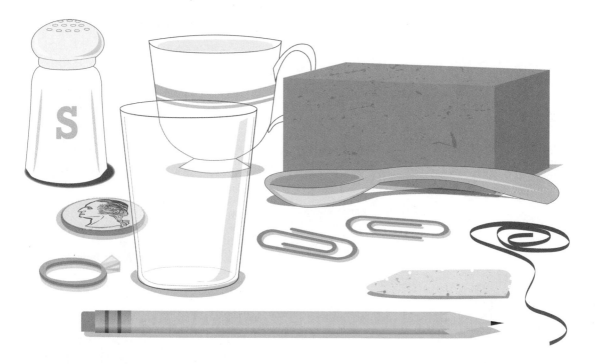

These items contain minerals. What did you find in your home and school?

4

How Hard Is That Mineral?

Things You Will Need:

- your fingernail
- steel nail
- paper and pencil
- chalk
- heavy copper wire (hardware store)
- glass
- sandpaper
- copper penny
- plastic

Scientists identify minerals by doing tests. One test measures a mineral's hardness. Of the things listed under "Things you will need," which one do you think is the hardest? The softest? Write down your ideas and your reasons for them.

Let's Investigate!

A harder object can scratch a softer one. Hardness is measured on Mohs' scale. This scale goes from 1 to 10. One is softest, and 10 is hardest. Your fingernail's hardness is between 2 and 3 on this scale. A steel nail is between 6 and 7.

1 On a piece of paper, write the numbers 1 to 10 from top to bottom. Leave space between the numbers. Write "fingernail" and "steel nail" in the correct places on your scale.

2 Can you scratch the chalk with your fingernail?

3 Can you scratch your fingernail with the copper wire?

4 Can you scratch the copper wire with the steel nail?

5 Can you scratch glass with the steel nail?

6 Can you scratch glass with sandpaper?

7 Add chalk, copper, glass, and sandpaper to your hardness list.

Do you think a copper penny will scratch your fingernail? Will it scratch a steel nail or glass? Will your fingernail scratch plastic?

How Hard Is That Mineral? The Facts

The Mohs' scale goes from the softest mineral (1), which is talc, to diamond (10), which is the hardest mineral. Diamond can scratch all other minerals. With the things you tested, you probably found the following order of hardness: chalk (softest), fingernail, copper, steel, glass, sandpaper (hardest). Chalk was less than 2 on the scale. It was softer than your fingernail. Copper was more than 2 but less than 6. Glass was greater than 6 because it could not be scratched by steel. Sandpaper was even harder than glass. The sand particles could scratch the glass.

1 chalk
2
3 fingernail
4 copper
5
6
7 steel
8 glass
9 sandpaper
10

You probably discovered that some plastics are softer than 2; others are harder.

Ideas for Your Science Fair

- Add other things to the hardness scale you developed in Experiment 4.

- Find out what other tests are used to identify minerals. Use one or more of them to identify minerals.

A Closer Look at Soil

Things You Will Need:

- trowel
- soil from several different places
- plastic cups
- water
- sheets of white paper
- warm place where soil can dry
- magnifying lens

What do you think you can find in soil? Write down your ideas and your reasons for them.

1 Use a trowel to collect some samples of soil from several different places.

2 Put the samples in plastic cups to take home.

3 Feel the soil samples. Do any feel gritty? Sticky? Smooth?

4 Pour water slowly into the cups that hold the soil. What do you observe? Do you see bubbles coming from the soil? What do you think might be causing the bubbles? Write down your idea and your reason for it.

5 Spread the wet soil samples on sheets of white paper. Let them dry for several days in a warm place.

6 When the soils are dry, use a magnifying lens to look at the soils. What do you see? Can you find particles that look like grains of sand or pieces of rock? Can you find old pieces of plants—leaves, bark, roots?

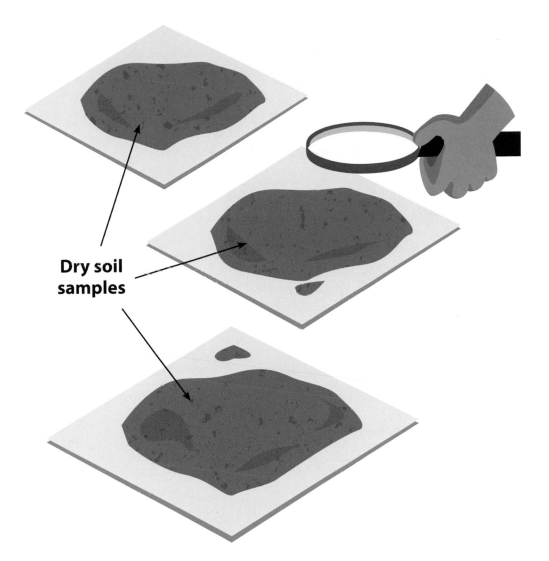

Dry soil samples

A Closer Look at Soil: *The Facts*

Most soils are layered. The top layer (topsoil) is usually dark. It contains the remains of living things—rotted leaves, bark, dead plants. Subsoils (the layers underneath) are usually lighter.

Air bubbles come out of soil
when water is added.

IN SOIL:

Solid pieces of rock   Pieces of decaying plants

All soils contain tiny particles that came from rocks. Sandy soil feels gritty. It has the largest soil particles. Silty soil feels smooth. Soil with lots of clay feels sticky. Its particles are very small.

When you added water to the soils, you probably saw bubbles of air. Air was between the soil particles. The water pushed the air out. Good topsoil contains air as well as particles of rocks and decaying plants.

Idea for Your Science Fair

- **What fraction of dry soil is actually air? Do an experiment to find out.**

6

Where Does Soil Come From?

Things You Will Need:

- variety of small rocks with cracks or rough surfaces
- water
- shallow container about 3 inches (8 cm) deep with tight-fitting cover
- a freezer

Where do you think soil comes from? Write down your ideas and your reasons for them.

Let's Investigate!

Weathering changes rocks to soil. This experiment is about one kind of weathering. There are many other kinds.

1 Find a variety of small rocks. Try to find rocks that have cracks or rough surfaces. Wash them with water to remove dirt.

2 Find a shallow plastic container that has a tight-fitting cover. Put the rocks in the container. Cover the rocks with water. Then put the tight-fitting cover on the container.

3 Place the container in a freezer. Be sure it is level so the rocks are covered with water. Leave the container overnight while the water freezes.

4 Remove the container and take off the cover. Let the ice melt. Then examine the rocks. Do you see any small particles of rock in the water? If so, where do you think they came from?

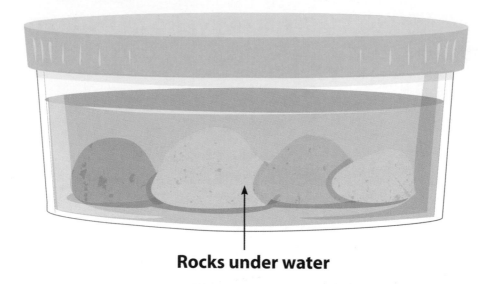

Rocks under water

5 Empty the water and any rock particles. Then repeat the experiment. Do this several times. Each time look for small rock particles after the ice melts.

Where Does Soil Come From? The Facts

Freezing is one way that rocks weather (break down). After one or more freezings, you probably saw small particles of rock in the water. When water freezes, it expands (gets bigger). As it expands, it can split rocks or break off small pieces. These small rock particles mix with organic matter (rotting leaves, grass, bark, and other plant parts) to make soil. The rock particles contain the minerals that plants need when they grow in soil.

This drawing shows how the acid in rain can change the minerals in some rocks into particles of soil.

Acid rain

Evaporation of water

Rock

Some chemicals in rock are carried away by acidic water.

Dissolved rock

Tiny particles of chemical in rock can now become part of the soil.

Ideas for Your Science Fair

- Do an experiment to show that water expands when it freezes (changes to ice).

- Do experiments to explain why ice floats in water.

- Freezing is one way that rocks are changed to soil. Do experiments to show other ways that rocks are broken up into soil.

7

What Is Igneous Rock?

Things You Will Need:

- an adult
- pie pan
- spray can of cooking oil
- stove
- spoon
- sugar
- measuring cup
- frying pan
- oven mitt
- measuring spoons
- baking soda
- salt
- vanilla
- refrigerator

"Igneous" comes from a Latin word meaning "fire." It is a good name for igneous rocks that are made deep inside Earth where it is very hot. It is so hot that rocks and minerals become a liquid called magma. Magma often pours onto the earth from volcanoes. When it comes from a volcano, it is called lava. The lava cools to become solid igneous rock.

How could you make a model to show how igneous rocks form? Describe your model on paper and explain how it would work.

Let's Investigate!

1 Spray a pie pan with cooking oil.

2 **Ask an adult**, wearing an oven mitt, to heat, with constant stirring, one cup of sugar in a frying pan. When all the sugar has turned to a golden syrup, the pan should be removed from the heat.

3 **Have the adult** quickly stir in 1/8 teaspoon of baking soda, 1/8 teaspoon of salt, and 1/2 teaspoon of vanilla.

4 **Have the adult** pour the very hot "lava" into the oiled pie pan. Let the "lava" cool to form hard "igneous rock."

5 After an hour, put the pan in a refrigerator. Later, remove the "rock" and crack it into pieces. Enjoy an "igneous rock" dessert.

What Is Igneous Rock? *The Facts*

Some magma cools slowly inside Earth. It forms plutonic igneous rock. Granite is a plutonic igneous rock. Because it cools slowly, its mineral crystals are very large.

Magma that escapes from a volcano cools faster. It forms volcanic igneous rocks, such as basalt, that have small crystals. Basalt makes up more than half of Earth's outer rock surface.

In your model, the melted sugar, baking soda, salt, and vanilla represented lava. After it was poured out of the volcano (frying pan), it cooled and hardened. The hardened sugar candy represents the volcanic rock that makes up much of Earth's crust.

Cooling "lava" to form igneous rock

8

What Is Sedimentary Rock?

Things You Will Need:

- garden soil
- sand
- gravel
- plastic container
- tall, clear, quart jar with lid
- water
- paper towel

- white bread, two slices
- whole wheat bread, three slices
- grape jelly
- peanut butter (If allergic, use apple butter.)

Water contains rock and soil particles. As water flows over Earth's surface, the particles may drop to the bottom of the water. They may settle, forming a layer of particles—a sediment. Over time, layers of sediment may form. The layers may harden due to the weight of layers above them, forming sedimentary rocks. How could you make models to represent sediments and sedimentary rocks? Write down your ideas and your reasons for them.

Let's Investigate!

1 Mix some garden soil, sand, and gravel in a plastic container. Fill a tall, clear, quart jar about one-third of the way with the mixture. Then nearly fill the jar with water.

2 Put the lid on the jar. Shake the jar for one minute.

3 Put the jar on a paper towel. Let the soil particles settle overnight to form a sediment. Where are the biggest particles? The smallest?

4 To make a model of sedimentary rocks, remove the crusts from slices of white and whole wheat bread. Stack the slices to make visible layers (see drawing at the bottom of this page). Spread peanut butter or apple butter between two slices. Spread jelly between two others. You have made a model of sedimentary rock. How is this model different from real sedimentary rock? Save your model for the next experiment.

Sediments

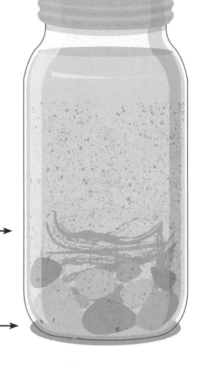

Smaller, lighter particles

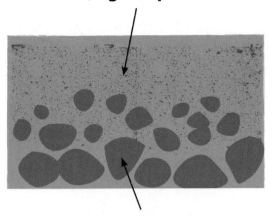

Larger, heavier particles

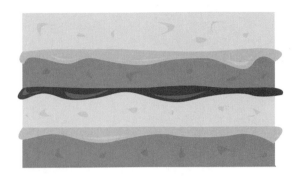

This model shows layers of sedimentary rock.

What Is Sedimentary Rock?
The Facts

Large, heavy particles such as gravel and sand settle out of water first. They fall through the water faster. Smaller, lighter particles of silt and clay fall more slowly. They settle on top. Over time, many layers of sediment settle on top of each other. The weight can cause the layers to harden and become sedimentary rock.

Your model has layers like sedimentary rock. However, sedimentary rock is much harder than bread. And, of course, it does not contain peanut butter or jelly. The peanut butter or apple butter might represent mud. The jelly could represent dissolved minerals that will turn solid as the water evaporates.

Ideas for Your Science Fair

- Make your own model to represent sedimentary rock.

- Fossils (remains or imprints of ancient plants and animals) are often found in sedimentary rocks. If there are fossils near your home, go on a fossil hunt with an adult. See if you can find and identify some fossils.

9

Taking a Core Sample

Things You Will Need:

- model from Experiment 8
- a plate
- clear, wide, plastic drinking straw

How do scientists know what kind of rocks and soil are under the ground? Write down your ideas and your reasons for them.

Let's Investigate!

1 Put the sedimentary rock model you made in Experiment 8 on a plate.

2 Find a clear, wide, plastic drinking straw. Put one end of the straw on the center of the rock model. Turn the straw very slowly and gently. Turn, do not push! As you turn the straw, it will slowly pass through the layers of "rock."

3 When the end of the straw reaches the plate, pull it up slowly.

4 Look at what is inside the straw. You have made a core sample of the rock model.

Can you identify each layer in the core? Can you tell which layer is deepest? Can you tell which layer is nearest the surface? Save the model for the next experiment.

Taking a Core Sample: *The Facts*

The lower end of the straw held the deepest layer of your "sedimentary rock." You could probably identify each layer

from top to bottommost. Could you also tell where the "mud" (peanut butter or apple butter) and crystals (jelly) were located?

Geologists get core samples by drilling into the earth. In that way they can tell what kinds of rocks are under the ground. This is how they locate coal, oil, and metal ores. Many metals are obtained from ores. For example, steel is made by heating iron ore with carbon and limestone in a blast furnace.

10

What Is Metamorphic Rock?

Things You Will Need:

- an adult
- model of sedimentary rock from Experiment 8
- aluminum foil

- three bricks or a stack of heavy books
- oven
- clock

Deep within the earth it is very hot and the pressure is very great. The pressure is caused by the tons of rocks and soil above. The heat and pressure can change sedimentary rock into another kind called metamorphic rock.

You can make a model to show how one kind of rock can be changed into another kind.

Let's Investigate!

1 Place your model of sedimentary rock from Experiment 8 on a sheet of aluminum foil. (The foil should be about three times as wide and long as the model.) Put another sheet of foil on top of the model.

2 Place three bricks or a large stack of books on top of the "rocks." Put this pressure on your "sedimentary rock" for about an hour.

3 Remove the weights. Completely wrap the pressurized model (bread) with the foil.

4 **Ask an adult** to heat the foil-covered "rock" in a 400-degree-Fahrenheit oven for about two hours.

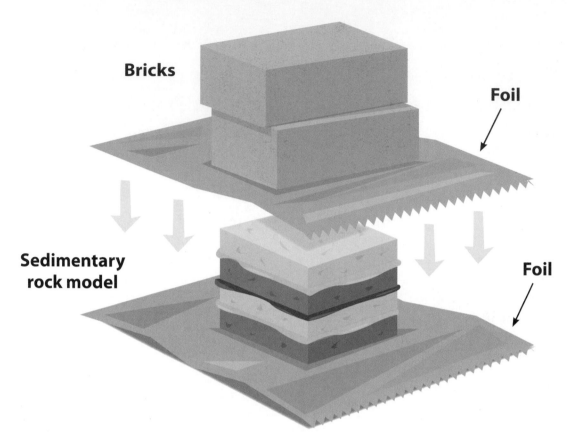

Bricks

Foil

Sedimentary rock model

Foil

5 **Ask the adult** to remove the foil-covered "rock" from the oven.

6 After the "rock" has cooled, open the foil. How has your "rock" changed?

What Is Metamorphic Rock?
The Facts

You put pressure on the sedimentary rock (layers of bread) by adding a heavy weight. Squeezing the "rock" with pressure made it smaller. Heating the "rock" made it harder and changed its color.

Similar things happen deep inside Earth where both pressure and temperature are very great. Pressure and heat can change a sedimentary rock such as limestone into marble, a metamorphic rock. Marble is used in making buildings such as museums or monuments.

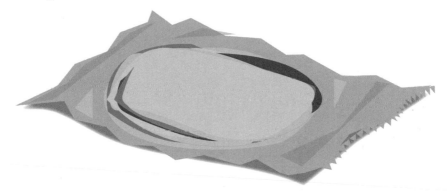

Ideas for Your Science Fair

- See how acid rain can affect marble buildings and statues. Pour some vinegar, a weak acid, onto some marble chips. (Your science teacher may have some.) What happens?

- Does vinegar affect limestone and chalk in the same way?

Glossary

acid rain Rain containing acidic substances (sour substances similar to vinegar).

crust The outermost layer of the earth.

crystals Solid minerals that have a distinct shape and a certain combination of chemicals.

igneous rock Rock formed from hot liquid minerals deep within the earth. The liquids harden when cooled to form igneous rock.

lava Magma that has reached Earth's outer surface.

magma Hot liquid minerals deep within the earth.

metamorphic rock Minerals or rocks that have been heated under pressure deep within the earth. The process can change sedimentary and igneous rock into metamorphic rock.

minerals Nonliving matter found in nature. Each type of mineral contains chemicals combined in a certain way.

plutonic rock Igneous rock formed inside Earth's crust where magma cools slowly.

rock A solid containing one or more minerals. There are three types of rocks: igneous, sedimentary, and metamorphic.

sediment Particles of rocks, soil, and other matter that settle out of water or air.

sedimentary rock Rock formed from sediments that have hardened over time.

volcanic rock Igneous rock formed from magma that flowed from a volcano.

Further Reading

Books

Ardley, Neil. *101 Great Science Experiments.* New York, NY: DK Ltd., 2014.

Buczynski, Sandy. *Designing a Winning Science Fair Project.* Ann Arbor, MI: Cherry Lake Publishing, 2014.

Hyde, Natalie. *Earthquakes, Eruptions, and Other Events that Change Earth.* New York, NY: Crabtree Publishing Co., 2016.

Latta, Sara. *All About Earth: Exploring the Planet with Science Projects.* North Mankato, MN: Capstone Press, 2016.

McGill, Jordan. *Earth Science Fair Projects.* New York, NY: AV^2 by Weigl, 2012.

Sohn, Emily. *Experiments in Earth Science and Weather.* North Mankato, MN: Capstone Press, 2016.

Websites

Mineralogical Society of America
minsocam.org/MSA/K12/K_12.html
This is a great website to learn about rocks and minerals.

NASA
climatekids.nasa.gov
NASA's Climate Kids: NASA's Eyes on the Earth is filled with links and games about air, weather, water, energy, plants, and animals.

Smithsonian Institution
gimizu.de/sgmcol
Take a look at the Smithsonian's gem and mineral collection.

Index